EASTER PUZZLES for KIDS

Activity Book

Scripture taken from the Holy Bible, NEW INTERNATIONAL VERSION®, NIV® Copyright © 1973, 1978, 1984, 2011 by Biblica, Inc.® Used by permission. All rights reserved worldwide.

The purchase of this coloring book grants you the rights to photocopy the contents for classroom use. Notice: It is unlawful to copy these pages for resale purposes. Copy permission is for private use only.

Copyright © 2025 Warner Press, Inc. All rights reserved. Made in USA

305800232025

People in the Easter Story

Do you remember these people from the Easter story and what they did?

Circle the words hidden forwards, backwards, up, down, or diagonally.

```
J S C T D P E O P M W H T F S Q J K J F H
O U I J R P E V X O H G Y Z E A W L D C E
H W W M H N V T Y G J W I Q M U K L A R M
N I O Q O U I X A E Y M Q E X G M E K A T
P Z H H X N Q E S L P Q S Z H E H S R A U
P J K N E G O U Y C I Y Q V L T C Y G V U
A Q Q X N V S F Z P F P E O A C M Q J J U
J L F V G T S F C W T H I M Q A W P X H B
D U P M S D R A T Y F K I B G R E W X E C
D E D S M A D R M Y R R B D M W A Y G A M
L J F A S R V Q I P A E A Y W W P S I W Y
G V M Z S J X X E F J L N S Q Z A A E O U
O M G U W I J S O G E U U E G D P F U A H
L H M O Q F A H F N Y M Z C S H V O Z A C
R V N I A B P D E I E S T P A U F S X K M
F M K V B E B J R D Y X Y S Z Q H E I W V
X Y M A S U Q P O J H N P E D D Z C R E X
G Q R O A O E C Y D M K O P E T E R L K E
U A J A R A I X R J I A S Z C R S A D A B
B N G T M N C U V B G S A N N A X O T V M
```

Jesus **Mary Magdalene** **Annas** **Judas**
Peter **Caiaphas** **James** **Pilate**
Mary **Simon of Cyrene** **Caesar** **Nicodemus**
John **Joseph of Arimathea** **Barabbas** **Malchus**

Jesus Enters Jerusalem

Jesus and His disciples were on their way to Jerusalem for Passover. This would be the last time Jesus would celebrate Passover with His disciples. The people along the road who welcomed Jesus believed they were cheering for an earthly king. They did not realize Jesus was their Savior.

*Use a NIV Bible to fill in the blanks.
Then use the words you wrote to complete the crossword puzzle.*

They took _____ _____ **and went out to meet him.**
(2 DOWN)
John 12:13 (NIV)

"_____ **is the** _____ **of** _____!" *John 12:13 (NIV)*
(6 ACROSS)   (15 DOWN)   (9 DOWN)

_____ **found a young** _____ **and sat on it.** *John 12:14 (NIV)*
(3 DOWN)   (16 ACROSS)

"**Go to the** _____ **ahead of you.**" *Luke 19:30 (NIV)*
(1 DOWN)

People _____ **their** _____ **on the** _____.
(12 DOWN)   (5 ACROSS)   (4 DOWN)
Luke 19:36 (NIV)

"_____ **in the** _____ _____!"
(10 ACROSS)   (11 ACROSS)   (7 ACROSS)
Mark 11:10 (NIV)

Jesus entered _____. *Mark 11:11 (NIV)*
(14 ACROSS)

"**This is Jesus, the** _____ **from** _____
(13 DOWN)   (8 DOWN)
in Galilee." *Matthew 21:11 (NIV)*

Answer on page 16

© 2025 Warner Press, Inc All rights reserved   E4899

Nicodemus Meets Jesus

One night, a Pharisee named Nicodemus went to visit Jesus. He wanted to get to know Jesus better. Jesus taught Nicodemus about the kingdom of God and what it means to be "born again." We cannot be born again on our own or by following rules. We are born again by believing Jesus is God's Son. We aren't reborn with a new body, but with a new spirit inside. Jesus gives us a new life on earth and a home in heaven with Him someday.

Write the letters from the puzzle pieces in the empty pieces that match in the cross. Then read what Jesus told Nicodemus.

Serving Others Like Jesus

During the Passover meal, Jesus got up, wrapped a towel around His waist, and filled a large bowl with water. Then He knelt down and began washing His disciples' feet. The disciples were surprised. Usually, a servant washed the guests' feet, not someone special like Jesus! They didn't understand why He would do such a thing. Jesus said He was giving them an example of what to do in the future. Just as Jesus served by washing their feet, they should serve others too.

Unscramble the letters. Then use the numbered letters to solve the code.

Ways I Can Serve:

Offer a **INHEGLP DAHN** — H E L P I N G H A N D
(1, 2, 3, 4 / 5, 6, 7, 8)

YARP ORF Others — P R A Y F O R
(9, 10, 11 / 12, 13)

WHOS God's **VELO** — S H O W L O V E
(14, 15, 16, 17 / 18, 19, 20)

SEU My **LENTTAS** — U S E T A L E N T S
(21, 22, 23 / 24, 25, 26, 27, 28, 29, 30)

"I, your Lord and Teacher, have washed your feet, **Y O U** (11, 19, 21) **A L S O** (10, 3, 22, 16) **S H O U L D** (14, 1, 13, 21, 26, 8) **W A S H** (17, 6, 30, 5) **O N E** (16, 7, 20) **A N O T H E R** (25, 4, 19, 29, 15, 27, 9) **' S F E E T** (14, 12, 23, 2, 24)."

John 13:14 (NIV)

The Last Supper

Before He died, Jesus took some bread and wine. He gave thanks, broke the bread, and gave the disciples some, saying, "This is my body given for you" (Luke 22:19 NIV).

Then He took the cup and said, "This cup is the new covenant in my blood, which is poured out for you" (Luke 22:20 NIV). We call this meal the Last Supper. When we share the bread and wine (or grape juice) at church, we call this "communion."

We remember all that Jesus did so that we can have eternal life with Him in heaven.

Write the first letter of each picture to see what Jesus told his disciples.

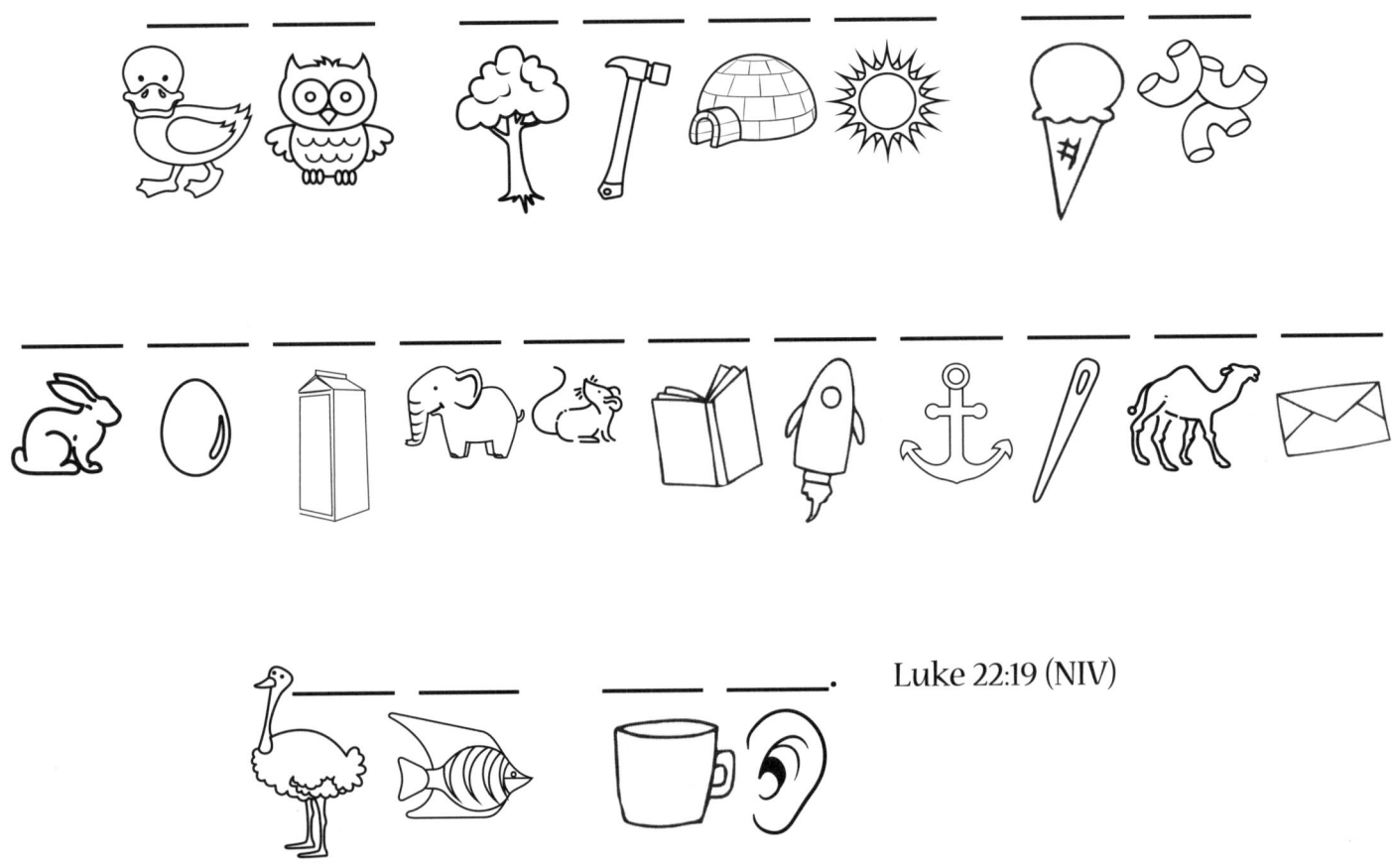

Luke 22:19 (NIV)

Jesus Prayed

Jesus knew the time was coming soon when He would die on the cross. He tried to prepare His disciples for what was about to happen, but they couldn't really understand. After He had taught them and shared the Passover meal with them, Jesus prayed. You can read His prayer in John 17.

Who did Jesus pray for?
Cross out every Q and Z. Then write the letters you have left in order on the blanks.

1. ___ ___ ___ ___ ___ ___

2. ___ ___ ___   ___ ___ ___ ___ ___ ___ ___ ___

3. ___ ___ ___ ___ ___ ___
   ___ ___ ___ ___ ___ ___ ___

Our prayers to God are very important. Who would you like to pray for today?

_____

Two Crowns

Jewish leaders took Jesus to Pilate to be judged. Pilate knew Jesus had done nothing wrong, but the Jews kept pressuring him to convict Jesus of a crime.

Pilate sent Jesus away to be beaten. Soldiers twisted together a crown of thorns and pushed it down on Jesus' head. They made Him wear a purple robe like a king would wear. Then they hit Jesus and mocked Him.

Because Jesus wore a crown of thorns and took our punishments, those of us who believe in Him will one day receive a heavenly crown.

What does the Bible say? Use the code to find out.

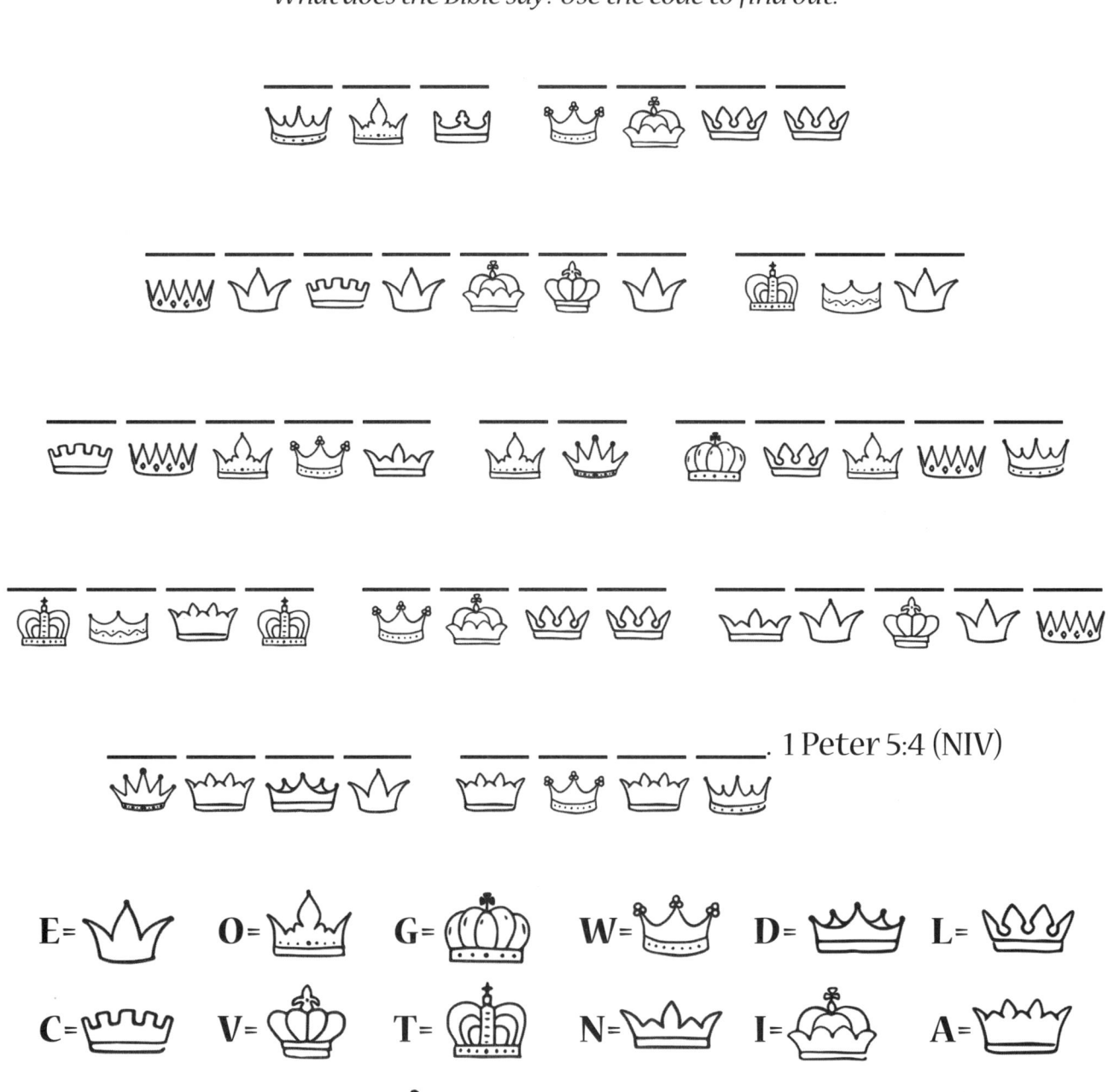

... 1 Peter 5:4 (NIV)

Peter Denies Jesus

After the Last Supper, Jesus talked to Peter. Jesus said He knew Peter was going to turn away from Him. Peter said, "Jesus, I will go to prison or even die with you." Jesus said, "Before the rooster crows today, you will deny Me three times." When Jesus was arrested, Peter followed at a distance. Three times people said they knew Peter had been with Jesus. Three times Peter said he didn't know Jesus. Just then, the rooster crowed. Peter realized he had disowned Jesus three times. He was so sorry for what he had done that he went away and cried.

Color the spaces with dots to see the picture.

The Cross

Being killed on a cross was a terrible way to die. The Romans used this painful method on people who were criminals, a threat to the government, or an enemy of their country. Jesus was crucified because the religious leaders felt threatened by His popularity and His teaching. God had planned for Jesus to die to save us from our sins. Through Jesus, we can confess our sins and be forgiven. The cross now has become a symbol of hope for Christians. Because Jesus died, we can live forever!

Help the kids find their way through the maze to Jesus. Try to avoid the sins along the way!

Answer on page 16

Jesus' Last Words

Even when Jesus was dying on the cross, He was thinking of others.
The Bible tells us about seven things Jesus said from the cross.
Jesus was in terrible pain, and it was very difficult for Him to speak at all. That fact makes these statements even more important for us to remember and think about.

Use a NIV Bible to fill in the blanks. Then use the words you wrote to complete the crossword puzzle.

"_____, _____ them, for they do not know what they are doing." *Luke 23:34 (NIV)*
   (6 ACROSS)   (9 DOWN)

"Truly I tell you, _____ you will be with me in _____." *Luke 23:43 (NIV)*
                     (13 DOWN)   (8 DOWN)

He said to her, "_____, here is your _____," and to the _____,
                  (1 DOWN)   (11 DOWN)   (15 ACROSS)
"Here is your _____." *John 19:26–27 (NIV)*
                (3 DOWN)

"My God, my _____, why have you _____ me?"
              (12 ACROSS)   (10 ACROSS)
Matthew 27:46 (NIV)

"I am _____." *John 19:28 (NIV)*
        (4 DOWN)

"It is _____." *John 19:30 (NIV)*
         (14 ACROSS)

"Father, into your _____ I _____
                    (5 ACROSS)   (2 ACROSS)
my _____." *Luke 23:46 (NIV)*
    (7 ACROSS)

Answer on page 16

Places in the Easter Story

Do you remember what happened at these places in the Easter story?

Circle the words hidden forwards, backwards, up, down, or diagonally.

```
M P H Z B A L W O F L K C C F Z O G Z U Y
N O O K C E P X Y C R G R O L J U O K I D
R D U F J T T R W X W O Y U Z J I G T M G
D W P N U S C H U Y S L D R I R W N G E T
N C H D T H R T A S G G J T M W F D T D F
J E R U S A L E M N J O Z Y J L Q H Y I K
A F P U G T I J I T Y T M A T X S S E P F
J J R J U N Y N A B G H C R W E S L M T S
L T A A E Y K M D S D A S D M E D O C Y V
K F E X S Z Z R F S C T E A V O N I G Z J
W Q T O T N B Y T H R B N I F O X G U X Z
E J O Y R Y I Z C U I E L B E N J Z A L J
G X R I O N H A O N V O L Q D G C N P B N
A X I W O U I C W O F O P E J Z A G F M N
H B U B M R E B A O O B S M E N F L V O H
P Y M L E L S U T D O F O D G L I Q L T K
H R Y H P J Z N Q H M Y R M L N I C V I C
T P X M S I U Q K Z B Z K I T E L L U F V
E Q E U C O F E N G J J Z Y D C I J A T J
B T A S M C B U R D Z J L J Y J E F E G D
```

Jerusalem   **Bethphage**   **Mount of Olives**   **village**
temple courts   **Bethany**   **Gethsemane**   **courtyard**
Field of Blood   **Praetorium**   **Golgotha**   **tomb**
mountain   **Galilee**   **fields**   **guest room**

An Angel with a Message

Jesus' friends were so sad that He was dead. His body was buried in a tomb with a huge stone blocking the door. Mary and Mary Magdalene were taking spices to put on Jesus' body. Suddenly, there was an earthquake. A bright angel dressed in white appeared, rolled away the stone, and sat on it! The angel said, "I know you are looking for Jesus. He is not here. He has risen!" The women were filled with joy. They ran quickly to tell the disciples that Jesus was alive!

Help the women reach the disciples with the good news!

Why Jesus Died

When we think about Easter and what Jesus did for us on the cross, we may wonder why Jesus gave up His life for people like us. Jesus never sinned in His whole life, and yet He was willing to die for our sins. Why would He do that? Because He loved us and wanted us to be saved.

Match the verse to the correct Scripture address and write the number in the blank circle. Use your NIV Bible if you need help.

Scripture Address	Verse
1. John 13:34-35 (NIV)	○ The reason my Father loves me is that I lay down my life—only to take it up again.
2. Galatians 2:20 (NIV)	○ Having loved his own who were in the world, he loved them to the end.
3. 1 John 4:9 (NIV)	○ Whoever has my commands and keeps them is the one who loves me. The one who loves me will be loved by my Father, and I too will love them and show myself to them.
4. Ephesians 3:17-18 (NIV)	○ Anyone who loves me will obey my teaching. My Father will love them, and we will come to them and make our home with them.
5. John 13:1 (NIV)	○ As I have loved you, so you must love one another. By this everyone will know that you are my disciples, if you love one another.
6. 2 Corinthians 5:14-15 (NIV)	○ Christ's love compels us, because we are convinced that one died for all…that those who live should no longer live for themselves but for him who died for them and was raised again.
7. 1 John 4:10 (NIV)	○ The life I now live in the body, I live by faith in the Son of God, who loved me and gave himself for me.
8. John 10:17 (NIV)	○ I pray that you, being rooted and established in love, may have power…to grasp how wide and long and high and deep is the love of Christ.
9. John 14:23 (NIV)	○ This is how God showed his love among us: He sent his one and only Son into the world that we might live through him.
10. John 14:21 (NIV)	○ This is love: not that we loved God, but that he loved us and sent his Son as an atoning sacrifice for our sins.

Easter Story Mix-Up

The events in Jesus' life that led to His death and resurrection are important for every Christian to remember. Jesus is God's only Son. God sent Him to earth to show the world His love, teach us the truth about God, and to save each person who believes in Him.

These pictures are all mixed up! Number the pictures correctly from 1-7 to tell the Easter story.

Answer on page 16

Answer Page

Page 2
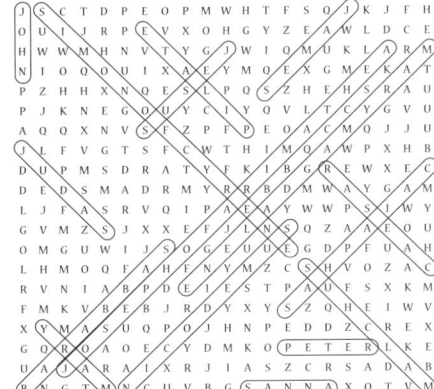

Page 3

Page 4

		F	O	R		G	O	D		
	S	O		L	O	V	E	D		
		T	H	E		W	O	R	L	D
T	H	A	T		H	E		G	A	V	E		H	I	S
O	N	E		A	N	D		O	N	L	Y		S	O	N
		T	H	A	T		W	H	O	E	V	E	R
B	E	L	I	E	V	E	S		I	N		H	I	M
			S	H	A	L	L		N	O	T
			P	E	R	I	S	H
			B	U	T		H	A	V	E
			E	T	E	R	N	A	L
			L	I	F	E	.		J	O	H	N
			3	:	1	6		(	N	I	V	)

Page 5
HELPING HAND, PRAY FOR, SHOW LOVE, USE TALENTS

you also should wash one another's feet

Page 6
Do this in remembrance of me.

Page 7
1. HIMSELF
2. THE DISCIPLES
3. FUTURE BELIEVERS

Page 8
You will receive the crown of glory that will never fade away.

Page 9

Page 10
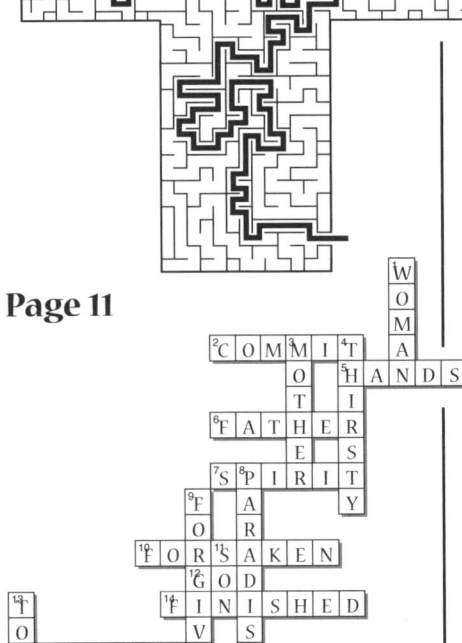

Page 11

Page 12
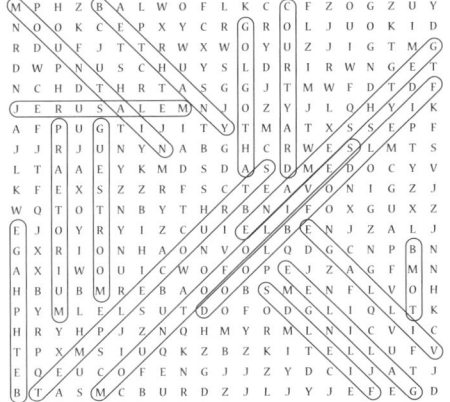

Page 13
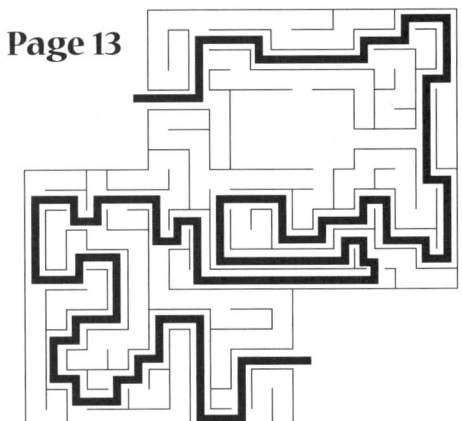

Page 14
Verses column: 8→6, 5→2, 10→4, 9→3, 1→7

Page 15
1. Jesus on a donkey
2. Jesus eats Last Supper
3. Jesus prays in garden
4. Jesus is arrested
5. Jesus on the cross
6. The tomb
7. Jesus rises to heaven